READ ABOUT

Insects

Anna Claybourne

COPPER BEECH BOOKS
BROOKFIELD • CONNECTICUT

Contents

© Aladdin Books Ltd 2000

Designed and produced by
Aladdin Books Ltd
28 Percy Street
London W1P 0LD

First published in
the United States in 2000 by
Copper Beech Books,
an imprint of
The Millbrook Press,
2 Old New Milford Road
Brookfield, Connecticut 06804

ISBN 0-7613-1215-3
Cataloging-in-Publication data is on file
at the Library of Congress.

Printed in U.A.E.

All rights reserved

Editor
Sarah Milan

Series Editor
Jim Pipe

Science Consultant
David Burnie

Series Literacy Consultant
Wendy Cobb

Design
Flick, Book Design and Graphics

Picture Research
Brooks Krikler Research

What Are Insects?

Insect Bodies • Types of Insects

An insect is a kind of animal. There are more insects in the world than any other kind of animal. For every person on Earth, there are at least a billion insects!

Insects live almost everywhere on Earth. There are insects that live in the air, under the ground, and even underwater.

The great diving beetle has an air supply stored under its wings.

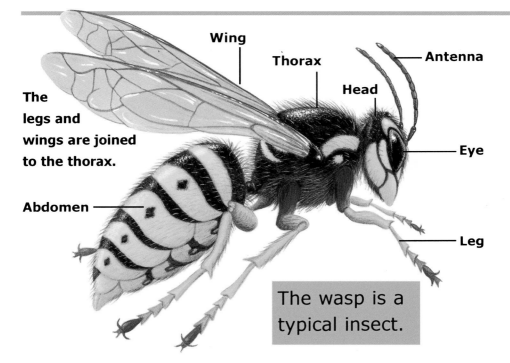

Wing

Thorax

Head

Antenna

The legs and wings are joined to the thorax.

Eye

Abdomen

Leg

The wasp is a typical insect.

All insects, once fully grown, have six legs. They have two feelers called antennae, which they use to feel and smell things.

An insect's body has three main sections — the head, the thorax (middle section), and the abdomen (tail section). Most insects have wings, but not all insects can fly. Some, like the wingless dog flea, jump instead.

This locust has grown too big for its old exoskeleton.

Insects don't have bones inside. Instead, they have a tough shell that surrounds them, called an exoskeleton.

As an insect grows, its exoskeleton becomes too tight. When a new one has grown underneath it, the insect gets rid of its old one. This is called molting.

Large animals need strong bones inside them to hold them up. Only small animals can have exoskeletons.

This giant stick insect is one of the biggest insects in the world. It is about twelve inches long. This picture shows its actual size.

Scientists think there are at least five million different types, or species, of insect. The reason there are so many is because, over millions of years, they have adapted to living in all sorts of different places.

Many insects live in your house! What are these houseflies eating? Answer on page 32.

There are a lot of small, creepy-crawly creatures that look like insects, but aren't. Spiders, centipedes, and woodlice aren't insects. They have too many legs. Slugs aren't insects either — they have no legs and their body is all in one section.

Insect Babies

Insect babies often look very different from their parents. They have to go through a lot of changes before they turn into an adult.

Most insects have babies by laying eggs. Before they can do this, they usually have to find a mate. But some insects, such as female aphids, can make babies on their own.

The female dragonfly lays her eggs in the water.

As they grow, insects go through stages. These stages are called a life cycle. A butterfly's life cycle has four main stages.

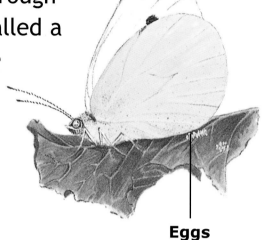

Eggs

1 Butterflies usually lay their eggs on a plant.

2 The eggs hatch into caterpillars. They have six legs at the front and about ten legs, called prolegs, at the back. Caterpillars spend all day munching plants.

Caterpillar

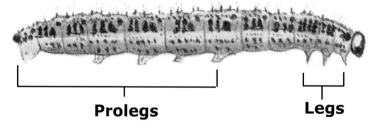

Prolegs   **Legs**

3 When a caterpillar is big enough, it goes through another stage and becomes a pupa. During this time, the adult organs are formed.

The pupa shuts itself away inside a hard case called a chrysalis (say "kri-sal-iss"). It doesn't eat or move around — it just changes. Over many weeks, it grows wings, long legs, and antennae.

Pupa inside chrysalis

4 At last, the pupa becomes a butterfly, tightly folded up inside its case. It wriggles and breaks free.

Butterfly emerging

Butterfly

We call this change metamorphosis (say "met-ah-mor-fo-siss"). Most insects, including beetles, bees, and flies, go through metamorphosis.

Some insects don't have a pupa stage. Their eggs hatch into babies called nymphs. As the nymphs grow, their skin splits and they wriggle out of it. This is called shedding their skin.

A baby shield bug has no wings. As it grows and molts, its wings start to grow.

Other kinds of insects don't lay eggs. They have living babies, which look just like their parents, but are much smaller. Like nymphs, they shed their skin as they grow bigger.

Newborn aphids look like a tiny version of their parents.

Honeybee larvae (babies) stay in the honeycomb while adult bees bring them food from outside.

Many insects go away or die after they have laid their eggs. Adult mayflies only live for one day. When their eggs hatch, the babies have to look after themselves.

Other insects, like honeybees and ants, spend a lot of time caring for their young. In a colony of ants, there are special "nurse" ants to feed and clean the larvae.

What Insects Eat

Just like other animals, there are insects that eat plants, and insects that eat other animals.

Lots of insects are plant-eaters, or herbivores. Bees and butterflies suck nectar from flowers. Locusts eat whole fields of farmers' crops.

Leafcutter ants cut off pieces from leaves with their scissorlike jaws. They carry them back to the nest to make a food store.

Leafcutter ants

We call an animal that eats other animals a carnivore. Most carnivorous insects kill and eat insects and other small creatures.

This spider wasp has caught a tarantula.

Spider wasps catch spiders to feed their young. They sting their prey so it can't move.

In a burrow, the female spider wasp lays an egg on top of a spider. When it hatches, the young spider wasp has a fresh supply of food!

A praying mantis feeds on a bee that it has just caught.

A praying mantis waits quietly with its front legs folded. Then, when a smaller insect passes by, the mantis suddenly grabs it.

The praying mantis gets its name from its two long front legs, which look like praying hands. For an extra meal, a female praying mantis eats the male she's just mated with!

Some insects are parasites. They feed on animals much bigger than themselves. Instead of killing their prey, they live on it.

Do you know where on your body this louse likes to live? Answer on page 32.

Lice are parasites that live on animals, including humans. When they are hungry, they bite their host (the animal they are living on) and suck out a bit of blood.

We call animals that eat both plants and animals omnivores. Insects that live in houses are often omnivores. We humans eat lots of different foods, and insects that live in our houses feed on our leftovers.

There are two main kinds of insect mouth. Some insects have strong jaws called mandibles that they use for chewing. Others have a mouth that they use for sucking.

Cockroaches hide in dark corners and come out to feed when no one is around.

Assassin bug

The assassin bug stabs its prey with its long, needle-sharp mouth. Then it injects a deadly spit that turns its victim's insides to jelly! It sucks up the jelly, leaving an empty shell.

Dragonfly nymph

A dragonfly nymph has a long stalk folded under its head. At the end of the stalk are grabbing jaws. As it crawls along on the river bed, the nymph uses its special mouth to reach out and grab tadpoles and small fish.

Staying Safe

Camouflage • Warnings • Insect Stings

Many animals feed on insects. Birds, lizards, fish, frogs, and even other insects all eat them. So insects have to find ways of hiding from danger. Here are some of their tricks.

To hide from hungry fish and frogs, caddis fly nymphs make themselves a hard case from twigs, pebbles, and other bits and pieces.

What is this case made of? Answer on page 32.

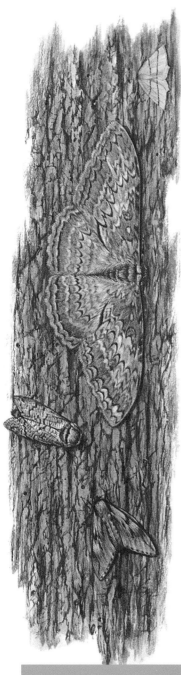

Many insects are hard to see. They look just like the plants they live on. This is a clever way to hide. We call it camouflage. It helps the insects to hide from their attackers.

This praying mantis looks like a pink flower.

Some moths look like the bark of a tree trunk. The leaf butterfly has wings that it folds. This makes it look like a dead leaf.

Can you spot four moths?

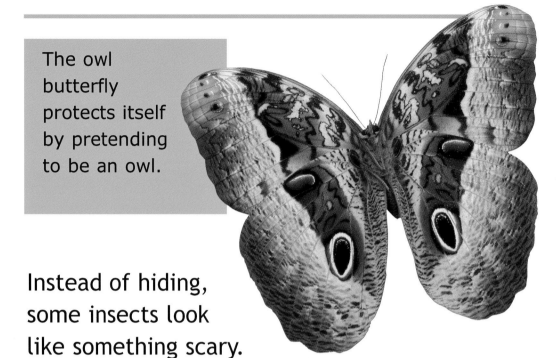

The owl butterfly protects itself by pretending to be an owl.

Instead of hiding, some insects look like something scary. Owl butterflies have a big spot on their wings. Each spot looks like a staring owl's eye. This frightens other animals away.

Bee hawkmoth

The bee hawkmoth looks like a bee, so other animals stay away, even though it can't sting.

But some insects really can sting. A wasp or bee sting hurts enough to scare even big animals like us away.

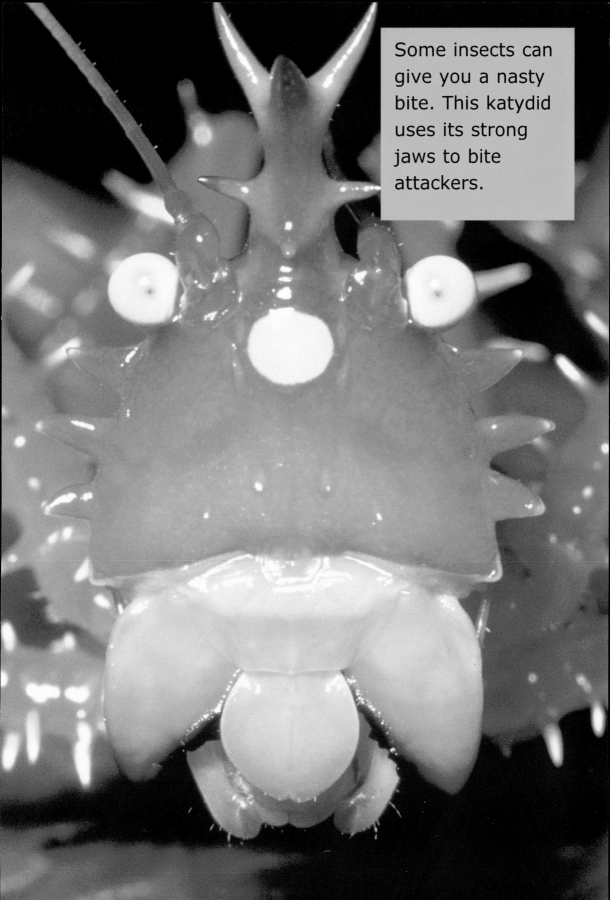

Some insects can give you a nasty bite. This katydid uses its strong jaws to bite attackers.

Some insects can even squirt poison. One kind of stick insect can squirt chemicals straight into its enemies' eyes. A bombardier beetle sprays its attackers with hot gas out of its bottom!

The gas that a bombardier beetle sprays at its attackers is both hot and irritating. This gives the beetle time to get away.

Living Together

What would it be like if you had to share your house with five million brothers and sisters? That's how termites live.

Termites in Africa built this tower from soil and their own spit.

Termites, ants, and some kinds of bees and wasps are social insects. They live together in a big group called a colony.

These insects share their food and help each other to survive.

Social insects usually build a home. Honeybees make a nest from wax and wasps build their nest from chewed wood.

In a colony of social insects, the members of the group all have different jobs to do. This is what happens in a large ant colony:

The most important member is the queen. Her job is to lay eggs — thousands of them.

An ants' nest has lots of rooms linked by tunnels. In the deepest and safest part is the queen.

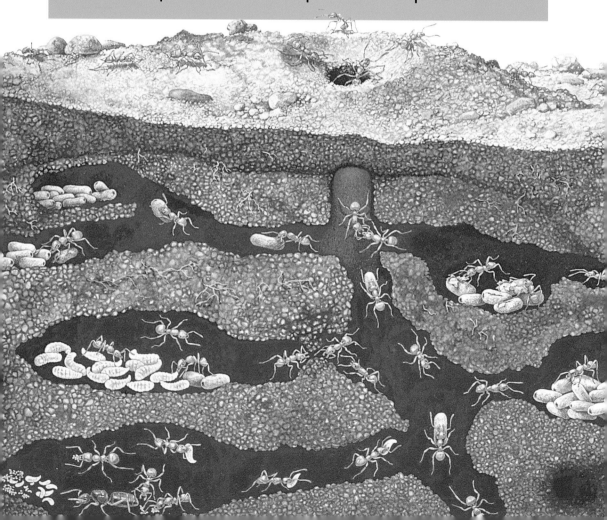

The queen of the colony is much bigger than the others. She can live for up to twenty years.

Most of the ants are female worker ants. They look after the queen, build and repair the nest, and collect food. They also look after the eggs and feed the babies when they have hatched.

Soldier ants attack a caterpillar.

The largest worker ants are the soldiers. Their job is to guard the colony. Male ants don't do any work in the colony. They live a short time and their only job is to mate with the queen.

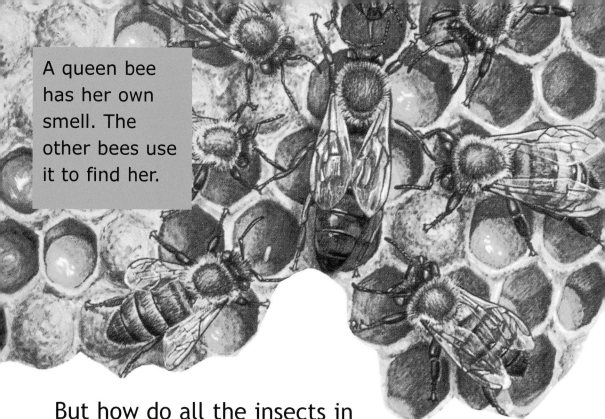

A queen bee has her own smell. The other bees use it to find her.

But how do all the insects in a colony know what to do and where to go? Like all animals, insects do some things without having to learn. When they are born, they know what to do. We call this instinct.

Social insects can also give each other messages using smells called pheromones (say "fer-ow-moans"). Honeybees can even tell each other when they have found a food supply by doing a special dance.

Bees use different dances for different messages.

Insects and Us

Insect Pests • Useful Insects

Insects can change our lives. Some cause problems for us: locusts eat our crops and mosquitos bite us and make us itch.

Cockroaches spread germs and look scary, so people don't want them in their home. Termites can be an even greater menace. They feed on wood and can cause damage to houses.

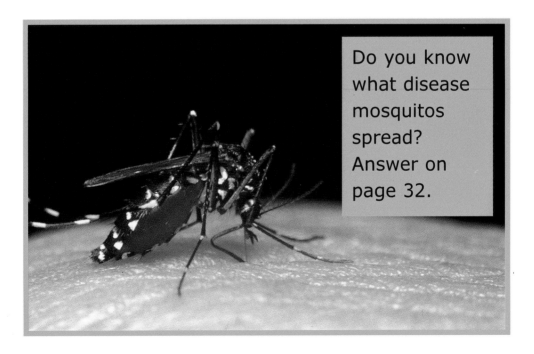

Do you know what disease mosquitos spread? Answer on page 32.

Some insects are very useful. We get honey from bees and silk from silkworms (the name for silkmoth caterpillars).

Insects can help farmers with pest control. Farmers buy ladybugs to eat aphids, so that the aphids can't eat their crops.

Silk comes from the cocoon (soft case) of the silkworm.

Insects are an important food for many other animals. If insects died out, animals like shrews and birds would starve.

Some people eat insects as a snack. This Aboriginal man in Australia is eating a moth caterpillar.

Insects are very important to plants, too. Bees, butterflies, and some beetles spread pollen from one flower to the next, so that the plants can make new seeds.

As they feed on a flower, the insects' legs and bodies get brushed by pollen. When they move on to the next flower, they leave some pollen on it. This is called insect pollination.

A beetle pollinates a flower.

Find Out More

PICTURE QUIZ

Billions of small creepy-crawlies live on our planet. Not all of them are insects. Do you know which of the creatures below are insects? Answer on page 32.

a Beetle   **b** Spider   **c** Scorpion   **d** Fly

UNUSUAL WORDS

Here we explain some words you may have read in this book.

Camouflage Colors or patterns that help an animal blend in with its background, making it hard to spot.

Caterpillar A baby moth or butterfly.

Exoskeleton The tough skin surrounding an insect that holds it together and protects it.

Larva (plural larvae) A kind of baby insect, such as a baby beetle or bee, that looks very unlike its parents.

Metamorphosis The changes that most insects go through before they become adult.

Molting This is when an insect grows out of its old skin after a new skin has grown beneath it.

Nymph A kind of baby insect that looks a bit like its parents and changes slowly into an adult by molting.

Pheromone A kind of smell that animals give out to send messages to each other.

Pupa The stage a baby insect goes through between being a larva and turning into an adult.

INSECT RECORDS

The longest insect is the giant stick insect. It grows up to 12 inches long (see pages 4-5).

The Australian Hercules moth *(right)* has the biggest insect wingspan — 11 inches.

The heaviest insect of all is the Goliath beetle *(left)*. It weighs about 4oz.

THE ANIMAL KINGDOM

This is the animal family tree. Examples of the main groups are shown. Can you see where insects belong?

ANIMALS WITH BACKBONES

Mammals	Birds	Reptiles	Amphibians	Fish

ANIMALS WITHOUT BACKBONES

MOLLUSKS

Snails	Clams	Octopuses

PRIMITIVE ANIMALS

SINGLE-CELL ANIMALS	SPONGES

STARFISH	JELLYFISH

ARTHROPODS

Spiders	Insects	Crustaceans

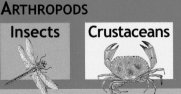

WORMS

31

Index

ANSWERS TO PICTURE QUESTIONS

Page 6 The houseflies are eating a donut.

Page 15 This louse lives in your hair and lays eggs called nits.

Page 18 The nymph's case is made of tiny shells.

Page 27 In some countries, female mosquitos can spread malaria.

Page 30 The beetle and the fly are both insects. The spider and the scorpion are not.

Photocredits: *Abbreviations: t – top, b – bottom, l – left, r – right.* Cover, back cover, and pages 6, 14, 17b, 21, 22, 23r, 27: Oxford Scientific Films; pages 3, 7, 16, 18, 28b, 29: Bruce Coleman Collection; pages 1, 20t: Stockbyte.
Illustrators: David Cook, Tony Swift, Myke Taylor, Philip Weare, Norman Weaver.